what about... dinosaurs?

what about...
dinosaurs?

Rupert Matthews

This 2009 edition published and distributed by:
Mason Crest Publishers Inc.
370 Reed Road, Broomall, Pennsylvania 19008
(866) MCP-BOOK (toll free)
www.masoncrest.com

Library of Congress Cataloging-in-Publication data is available

What About...Dinosaurs
ISBN 978-1-4222-1558-6

What About ... - 10 Title Series
ISBN 978-1-4222-1557-9

Printed in the United States of America

First published in 2005 by Miles Kelly Publishing Ltd
Bardfield Centre, Great Bardfield, Essex, CM7 4SL

Copyright © 2005 Miles Kelly Publishing Ltd

Editorial Director Belinda Gallagher
Art Director Jo Brewer
Editor Rosalind McGuire
Assistant Editors Lucy Dowling, Teri Mort
Design Concept John Christopher
Volume Designer Tony Collins
Picture Research Manager Liberty Newton
Picture Researcher Laura Faulder
Indexer Jane Parker
Reprints Controller Bethan Ellish
Production Manager Elizabeth Brunwin
Reprographics Anthony Cambray, Liberty Newton, Ian Paulyn

All images from the Miles Kelly Archives

CONTENTS

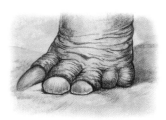

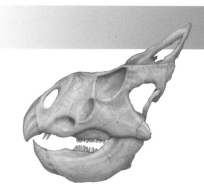

Bony Dinosaurs

Which dinosaur had the most armor?
How did *Ankylosaurus* live?
How did *Ankylosaurus* defend itself?
What were the bone-head dinosaurs?
Which was the smallest bone-head dinosaur?
Why did bone-heads have such thick skulls?

Cretaceous Hunters

Did dinosaurs hunt in packs?
Which was the brainiest dinosaur?
Which dinosaur ate fish?
Which dinosaur is called the "Mystery Killer"?
What was the "Terrible Claw"?
Which hunters had no teeth?

Tyrannosaurus rex

What did *Tyrannosaurus rex* look like?
How fast could *Tyrannosaurus rex* move?
What dinosaurs did *Tyrannosaurus rex* eat?
Why were its arms so small?
Why was its skull so strong?
Was *Tyrannosaurus rex* the biggest hunter dinosaur?

The End of the Dinosaurs

What was the world like just before the extinction?
Did the dinosaurs die out all at once?
Could a meteor have killed the dinosaurs?
Did volcanoes have an effect?
Could mammals have wiped out the dinosaurs?
What happened after the dinosaurs?

inosaurs lived on Earth many millions of years ago and none survives today. We know about dinosaurs because their bones have been preserved as fossils in rocks. Scientists have excavated thousands of dinosaur fossils and studied them with great care. By examining the fossils, scientists can tell what the dinosaurs looked like and how they lived. The scientists who study dinosaur and other ancient animal and plant fossils are called paleontologists.

Where can I meet a dinosaur?

In a museum of natural history. Many museums have complete skeletons of dinosaurs mounted so that they are in lifelike poses. These show how large the dinosaurs were when they were alive and the sorts of actions they could make. Some dinosaurs could run very quickly, or even leap in the air. Others were able to walk only very slowly.

What is a fossil?

An object from millions of years ago that has been preserved in rock. Most fossils are of bones or teeth because these hard objects are preserved more easily than soft skin or muscles. Over millions of years the original objects rot away and are replaced by minerals from the surrounding rocks. The fossils can be very heavy and are often fragile as well. Sometimes rare fossils of skin or muscles are found.

⬆ *Fossils are preserved in rock and are often displayed as they were found.*

⬆ *Some fossils are extracted from the rock and mounted as they would have been in life.*

Dinosaur **discoveries**

Key **dates**

1676   Robert Plot of Oxford publishes a book containing pictures of strange giant bones found in England.

1824   The first dinosaur to be named in scientific literature, *Megalosaurus* by Dr. William Buckland.

1842   British scientist Dr. Richard Owen uses the word "dinosaur" for the first time to describe three different large ancient reptiles.

1854   Concrete model dinosaurs are erected at London's Hyde Park—they are now in Crystal Palace.

1933   The Hollywood movie *King Kong* shows humans and dinosaurs together, although all dinosaurs died long before humans evolved.

10 famous fossil **finds**

1822   Dr. Gideon Mantell discovers the first dinosaur fossils in Sussex, England. They belong to *Iguanodon*.

1858   Joseph Leidy discovers the first dinosaur skeleton in New Jersey. It is a *Hadrosaurus*.

1878   Coal miners at Bernissart in Belgium discover 40 complete *Iguanodon* skeletons.

1909   Earl Douglass discovers the largest known find of fossils in the world, in Utah. It is now Dinosaur National Monument and is still being excavated.

1925   Dinosaur nests and eggs are discovered for the first time by Roy Andrews digging in the Gobi Desert in central Asia.

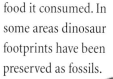

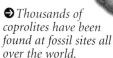

An excavation in the field. Each fossil must be carefully recorded, together with the precise place where it was found.

Where are dinosaur fossils found?

In Mesozoic rocks. These date to the time of the dinosaurs—230 to 65 million years ago. When a dinosaur died its bones might have become covered by sand or sunk into mud. This might then have become buried and turned to stone. When these rocks are lifted to the surface by earthquakes or erosion, the fossils can be found and excavated.

In the laboratory specialists carefully remove the fossils from the rock.

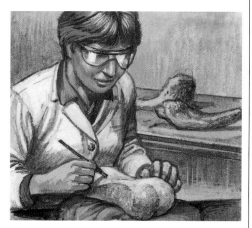

Fossils are cleaned to ensure that even the smallest details can be seen.

How are fossils prepared for study?

By cleaning them. The paleontologist must remove the fossil from the surrounding rocks, called the matrix. Some types of rock can be dissolved away with chemicals, but most need to be scraped away with metal hooks and chisels. Some paleontologists like to use a dentist's drill to remove final traces of rock. The fossils are then often soaked in chemicals to make them less fragile. Finally, they are photographed and drawn in detail.

How do scientists study fossils?

By comparing them to the bones of other animals. Paleontologists search for animals that have teeth of a similar shape to those of the fossil. If the two animals have similar teeth, they probably ate similar foods. The marks left on bones by muscles show how strong the dinosaur was and in which direction it could move its legs, neck, and other parts of its body.

Which are the most fragile fossils?

The most delicate dinosaur fossils are coprolites, the remains of dinosaur droppings. Fossilized droppings are known as coprolites and can reveal to scientists what the dinosaur had been eating, and how much food it consumed. In some areas dinosaur footprints have been preserved as fossils.

Thousands of coprolites have been found at fossil sites all over the world.

1969	Fossils of *Deinonychus* are found by John Ostrom, showing that some dinosaurs were fast, agile creatures.
1974	Hundreds of fossils are found in a remote area of Xigong Province, China. Most belong to previously unknown types of dinosaur.
1993	The largest dinosaur, and largest land animal, is discovered. *Argentinosaurus* may have weighed up to 100 tons.
1995	Discovery of fossils of the 50 ft. long *Giganotosaurus*, the largest meat-eating animal ever to walk the earth.
1998	The discovery of *Caudipteryx* in Liaoning, China, shows that some smaller dinosaurs were covered with feathers.

Naming **dinosaurs**

All dinosaurs have two names. The first is the genus name, and is the one used most often. The second name is a specific name and is rarely used.

If scientists discover a new type of dinosaur, they can name it after anything they like, except themselves.

Many dinosaurs have the ancient Greek word "saurus" as part of their name—it means "reptile" or "lizard."

Scientists sometimes change their minds about dinosaur names. The dinosaur *Brontosaurus* is now called *Apatosaurus*.

Iguanodon *hands could grip plants or act as a foot.*

The name "dinosaur" means "terrible lizard." This name was given to this group of animals in 1842 by the scientist Richard Owen. The dinosaurs were a group of reptiles closely related to the crocodiles, which held their legs underneath their bodies, like modern mammals. They are recognizable because some features of their skull bones are unlike those of any other type of reptile. It is thought that birds are probably descended from one type of dinosaur.

Why are dinosaur hips important?

All dinosaurs belong to one of two groups, which are divided by the shape of their hip bones. The saurischian dinosaurs had hip bones shaped like those of modern reptiles—the name "saurischian" means "reptile-hip." The ornithischian dinosaurs had hip bones that resemble those of modern birds—"ornithischian" means "bird-hip." These two groups are divided into smaller groups known as orders, within which are families of similar dinosaurs.

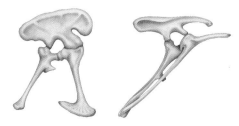

⬆ *The saurischian (left) had hips like modern reptiles. The ornithischian (right) had hips more like those of modern birds.*

⬇ *A scene from the late Cretaceous Period (around 100–65 million years ago). Success stories included the hadrosaurs or duck-billed dinosaurs, whose fossils have been found by the thousands.*

How many types of dinosaur were there?

Hundreds of different types of dinosaur have been named by scientists, but nobody is certain how many there were. Some different types of dinosaur are very similar, so some scientists think they should be put together as just one type of dinosaur. Other scientists believe that different fossils that are said to belong to only one type, should belong to several. There are thousands of dinosaur fossils that remain buried and have not yet been discovered.

Dinosaur **families**

Family groups
The dinosaurs are grouped together into families of similar creatures. The Ornithischia are divided into Ceratopsids, Pachycephalosaurids, Ankylosaurids, Nodosaurids, Stegosaurids, Hadrosaurids, Iguanodontids, and Ornithopods. All these animals were plant-eaters. The Saurischia were divided into two large groups. The Sauropods were the largest dinosaurs of all and were plant-eaters. The Theropods were two-legged meat-eaters. The Theropods are subdivided into smaller families, such as Tyrannosaurids, Spinosaurs, Dromaeosaurs, Ornithomimids, Oviraptosaurs, and others.

➡ *Scientists have found fossilized nests of* Maiasaura, *showing how the mother fed her young.*

Were all dinosaurs large?

No, a number of types of dinosaur were quite small. The hunting dinosaur *Compsognathus* was the smallest. It was about the same size as a modern chicken and weighed around 5.5 pounds. *Compsognathus* had a long tail and neck, so it may have reached over 3 ft. in length, but would have stood only about 16 in. tall. *Compsognathus* was a speedy hunter of little creatures such as insects, worms, and small lizards.

How large were dinosaur eggs?

Different dinosaurs laid eggs of varying sizes, depending on how large the adult dinosaur was. The smallest dinosaurs laid eggs that were about 1.5 in. long, or perhaps even smaller. The largest dinosaurs laid the largest eggs that have ever existed. They were about 16 in. across, or almost as large as a basketball, and were probably laid by sauropod dinosaurs.

○ *Dinosaur eggs varied greatly in size and in shape with some being smaller than a modern hen's egg.*

○ *The remains of embryonic dinosaurs have been found within a few fossilized eggs.*

How did dinosaurs have their young?

They laid eggs, which hatched into baby dinosaurs. Because eggs are fragile, they do not often become fossils. However, scientists have found a few fossilized eggs. These show that dinosaur eggs were shaped rather like modern crocodile eggs. Most were long and oval in shape, but the eggs of giant sauropod dinosaurs may have been round.

○ *Hunting dinosaurs were able to track other creatures, so they were probably about as intelligent as modern wild dogs.*

Were dinosaurs stupid?

Some dinosaurs had very small brains and were probably unintelligent, but others had fairly large brains and were quite bright. The hunter *Deinonychus* from North America was an intelligent dinosaur that could even cooperate with other dinosaurs when it was hunting.

○ *The fastest dinosaurs could easily have kept up with the fastest modern animals.*

How fast could dinosaurs run?

One family of dinosaurs were able to run very fast, perhaps at over 50 mi./hr. These ornithomimids looked similar to ostriches, and could run just as fast. They had lightweight bones and slim bodies, but very long, powerful rear legs. One genus, *Struthiomimus*, was about 11 ft. long and had longer legs than any other ornithomimid. It was probably the fastest dinosaur of all.

Key dates

Dinosaur family life spans
All dates are approximate

Millions of years ago	Family	Millions of years ago	Family
220–160	Prosauropods	110–65	Ankylosaurids
190–65	Sauropods	110–65	Ornithomimids
180–65	Nodosaurids	105–65	Pachycephalosaurids
170–80	Stegosaurids	100–65	Ceratopsids
150–80	Spinosaurs	95–65	Hadrosaurids
140–65	Iguanodontids	85–65	Oviraptosaurs
125–65	Dromaeosaurs	80–65	Theropods

Dinosaurs were not the first animals to exist on Earth. Creatures had been living and evolving for millions of years before the dinosaurs existed. Animals first appeared in the water, but they later evolved so that they could survive on dry land. The reptiles began to dominate life on land soon after they evolved. There were lots of different types of reptile all competing against each other to survive. The scene was set for the dinosaurs to emerge.

When did fish first evolve?

Around 450 million years ago. The first fish had skeletons of cartilage instead of bone, and lacked jaws. They probably fed on microscopic plants or animals. By 430 million years ago, fish had both bony skeletons and jaws. This made them better swimmers and allowed them to hunt larger creatures for food. All later vertebrates are descended from these early fish. The possession of two eyes and limbs arranged in pairs originated with these earliest creatures.

What were the ancestors of land animals?

The Coelacanth fish, which first appeared about 390 million years ago. It had fins that were very strong and muscular. These are known as lobe-finned fish, or Coelacanth, and would eventually evolve into land animals. It was originally thought that the Ceolacanth died out around 70 million years ago, but in 1933 one was caught off Madagascar. At the time it was thought that the Coelacanth must be extremely rare, but the local fishermen said they had been catching the creature for many years without realizing that it was anything special. It is now known that these fish can be found in deep waters of the Indian Ocean, although they are endangered and so their numbers are not huge.

⊙ The Coelacanth fish was for many years known only from ancient fossils, but scientists now know that it has survived in deep ocean waters to the present day.

Ancient **survivors**

Amazing **facts**

- The oldest known rocks are about 3.9 billion years old.
- Frogs have lived on Earth for 240 million years.
- The tuatara of New Zealand is the only survivor of the Rhynchosaur group of reptiles which evolved about 240 million years ago.
- Sharks appeared 400 million years ago and have changed little since.
- The horseshoe crab of North America has barely changed for 430 million years.

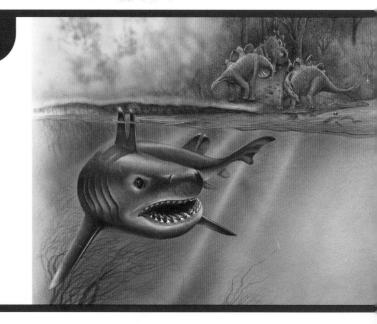

➔ Sharks cruised the waters of the seas when dinosaurs walked the Earth, and remain little altered to the present day.

⬆ *The ammonites were one of the most successful groups of sea creatures. They survived for millions of years, but are now completely extinct.*

➡ *The therapsid reptiles were covered with fur or hair and would have looked very much like modern mammals, though under the skin they remained very much ancient reptiles. Their descendants later became mammals.*

What were other sea animals like?

They were of many different shapes and sizes. Among the most common were the ammonites, which are closely related to modern squids and octopus. Ammonites first appeared around 330 million years ago. They had long, coiled shells filled with air that helped them to float, while tentacles helped them to catch small animals. Some later ammonites had straight or curved shells. All the ammonites died about about 65 million years ago, at the same time as the dinosaurs.

➡ *Reptiles had hard skin covered in scales that is impervious to water, and four limbs, though some forms walked on their hind legs only and used their front limbs as arms.*

When did the first reptiles live?

About 310 million years ago. Reptiles evolved from amphibians to become more suited to life on land. They laid hard-shelled eggs that could protect their young on land and had tough skin that prevented their bodies from drying out. *Dimetrodon* lived about 270 million years ago in North America. This reptile was about 10 ft. long and hunted other reptiles. It had a large sail of skin along its back that helped it to heat up its body in warm sunshine. Several other reptiles have evolved a similar sail of skin to help regulate their temperatures, including the dinosaur *Spinosaurus*.

What were the ancestors of mammals?

The therapsid mammals that appeared on Earth around 260 million years ago. These reptiles evolved into many different forms over the next 120 million years. Some therapsids were plant-eaters, others hunted other animals. They gradually evolved features such as hair and specialized jaw muscles. Some time before 200 million years ago one group of small therapsids evolved into mammals. These creatures survived through the age of the dinosaurs, then spread rapidly and evolved into a wide variety of forms.

Key dates

4.6 billion years ago	Earth forms from a mass of space dust and gas.
3.3 billion years ago	First simple plants, algae, begin to appear in the world's oceans.
700 million years ago	First water animals appear—worms, jellyfish, and sponges.
450 million years ago	First fish evolve in the oceans.
380 million years ago	Plants and insect-like animals move onto land.
330 million years ago	First amphibians evolve from fish and begin to live on land for part of their lives.
310 million years ago	One group of amphibians evolves into reptiles.
230 million years ago	First dinosaurs evolve.
220 million years ago	Small group of the therapsid reptiles evolve into mammals.

⬆ *The Earth formed from a mass of dust over millions of years.*

The dinosaurs first appeared on Earth, around 230 million years ago in South America. At this time, they were just one of many types of reptile. They quickly spread across the world and evolved into a large number of different species. The dinosaurs became the dominant animals on Earth, and they remained so for over 160 million years.

Which was the first dinosaur?

One of the oldest known dinosaurs was *Herrerasaurus,* which lived in South America about 230 million years ago. It was about 13 ft. long and hunted other animals. It had jaws filled with sharp teeth, which curved backwards. These would have been able to grip struggling prey and stop them from wriggling free. The jaws were powered by extremely strong muscles that would have been able to inflict a strong bite on any creature unfortunate enough to be caught by this predator. *Herrerasaurus* may have been the ancestor of the later sauropod dinosaurs, or of the theropods. There were also other dinosaurs living at about this time—scientists have found the fossils of a smaller predator, *Eoraptor.*

❯ Herrerasaurus *belonged to a group of large, powerful hunting reptiles. The first dinosaurs may have evolved from this group.*

What were the ancestors of dinosaurs like?

Dinosaurs belong to a group of reptiles known as the archosaurs, which means "ruling reptiles." This group includes crocodiles and several types of reptiles that are now extinct. *Ornithosuchus* was an early archosaur that may have been related to the ancestors of the dinosaurs. It was about 13 ft. long and was a hunter with powerful muscles.

Which was the first numerous dinosaur?

Coelophysis is a dinosaur that has been found in vast numbers. Hundreds of fossilized *Coelophysis* have been excavated in North America. The most dramatic find came in 1947 at the Ghost Ranch in New Mexico. Scientists found the fossils of an entire pack of these animals, almost 100 strong. The pack included *Coelophysis* of different ages from young to adult. The adults were about 10 ft. long with powerful hind legs and shorter front legs equipped with sharp claws. It is thought the pack was killed by a sandstorm.

Dinosaur **identification**

Four ways to identify a **dinosaur**

1   Legs are held directly under the body, not sprawling sideways as in other reptiles.
2   Ankle has a simple joint allowing only limited movements, unlike most reptiles that have ankles able to twist in all directions.
3   Hips are joined solidly to the backbone, not loosely as is more usual in reptiles.
4   Long hind legs. Nearly all dinosaurs had hind legs that were clearly longer than their front legs.

❯ *This fossilized skeleton of bones from a sauropod dinosaur shows the simple ankle joint that allowed the foot to move forward and back only. Other reptiles had more complicated joints.*

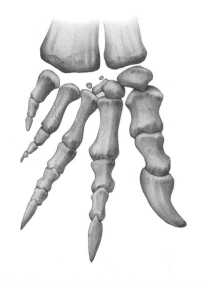

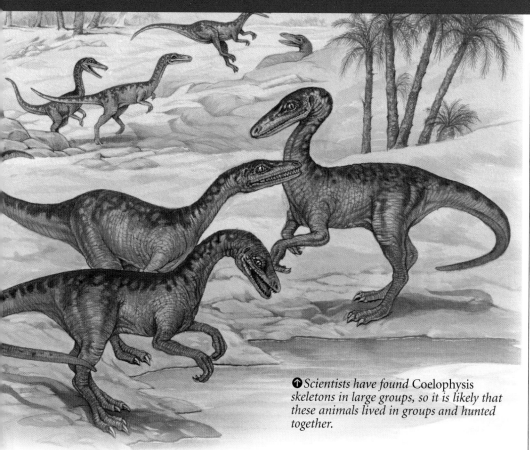

↑ *Scientists have found Coelophysis skeletons in large groups, so it is likely that these animals lived in groups and hunted together.*

Was there a link between crocodiles and dinosaurs?

The very earliest Archosaur reptiles would have been the ancestors of both crocodiles and dinosaurs. *Erythrosuchus* lived about 250 million years ago in southern Africa. It grew to be about 15 ft. long and was able to run fairly quickly when hunting other reptiles. The jaws were filled with dozens of sharp conical teeth, which were used to attack other animals. *Erythrosuchus* and similar animals already had the longer hind legs that were to become characteristic of almost all the later dinosaurs and crocodiles.

↓ *Coelophysis was one of the most agile of the early dinosaurs. It used its speed to hunt lizards and other small animals, which it then tore apart with its teeth and claws before eating them.*

How did *Coelophysis* live?

Coelophysis **hunted plant-eating dinosaurs and other animals.** It was able to run fast, while its long tail helped to balance the body as it changed direction at high speed. *Coelophysis* may have also hunted smaller animals such as lizards. One fossilized *Coelophysis* was found with a baby *Coelophysis* in its stomach, so this dinosaur must have eaten its own kind. This is called cannibalism and is extremely rare in animals.

It is not clear if *Coelophysis* ate its own kind as part of its usual diet or if this was strange behavior. The fossil was found in what was then a desert, so the adult animal may have eaten the younger only because there was a shortage of food. Not until scientists find more evidence will we be sure of the truth.

Key dates

Millions of years ago

300	First Diapsid reptiles appear.
260	First Archosaur reptiles evolve from Diapsid ancestors.
250	First crocodiles evolve from Archosaur ancestors.
235	First dinosaurs evolve from Archosaur ancestors
232	The reptile *Eoraptor* lived in South America; it may have been a dinosaur or an ancestor of dinosaurs.
230	Oldest known animal accepted as a dinosaur, *Herrerasaurus*, lives in South America.

↑ *The early Diapsid reptiles were heavy, robust four-legged reptiles. They could move only slowly and were very different from the later dinosaurs.*

The largest dinosaurs of all were the sauropods, which were also the largest land animals that have ever lived. All sauropods were saurischian dinosaurs and had a similar body structure. They had large bodies supported by four pillar-shaped legs. A small head was set on the end of a long neck, while a long tail was held out behind. Strong tendons ran between the neck and tail to help lift both clear of the ground.

Which was the biggest dinosaur?

The most massive dinosaur was probably *Argentinosaurus*, which lived in South America about 100 million years ago. Although scientists have found only parts of the skeleton, they think that the complete animal was about 130 ft. long and may have weighed up to 100 tons. This would make *Argentinosaurus* one of the largest animals that has ever lived.

How did sauropods live?

Scientists believe that the sauropods lived in herds of up to 30 animals. Fossilized footprints have been found that show numbers of sauropods all moving together in the same direction. The smaller, younger animals were in the middle of the

Which was the longest dinosaur?

Seismosaurus was about 150 ft. long and was probably the longest dinosaur of all. The name *Seismosaurus* means "earthquake lizard"—it was given to this animal because the scientist who discovered it thought that the ground would shake as it walked. *Seismosaurus* was similar to *Diplodocus*. These diplodocid dinosaurs lived worldwide in the Jurassic Period but later only in eastern Asia.

⬆ *Sauropods such as the* Argentinosaurus *were the largest of all the dinosaurs, and the largest land animals that ever lived.*

➔ Seismosaurus *had an extremely long, thin neck and an even longer tail. This made it the longest animal ever to walk on the Earth.*

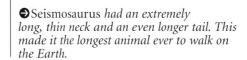

Through the ages

⬇ Stegosaurus *lived in the Jurassic Period, alongside the largest sauropods.*

Key dates

Millions of years ago

251	Start of Mesozoic Era, the Age of Dinosaurs.
251–200	The Triassic Period, the first of three periods of the Mesozoic Era. Some scientists date the Triassic as 240 to 210 million years ago.
200–145	Jurassic Period, the second of the periods of the Mesozoic Era. Some scientists date the Jurassic as 210 to 145 million years ago.
145–65	Cretaceous Period, the third of the periods of the Mesozoic Era.

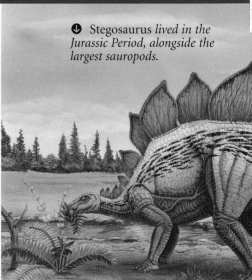

group so that they could be protected from hunting dinosaurs. When no danger was near, the herd of sauropods would have spread out to find food, although they would have needed to remain alert for danger.

Why are the names of some dinosaurs changed?

Scientists can sometime make mistakes when describing fossils, so the names of dinosaurs sometimes have to be changed. For instance, in 1985 an American scientist discovered the remains of a huge sauropod that he named *Ultrasaurus*. Before he could register the name, a Korean scientist used it for a different dinosaur, so the American registered the name

Ultrasauros instead. A few years later he realized that his *Ultrasauros* was really just a large *Brachiosaurus*, so the name was dropped completely.

Decisions about what name can be used to describe a dinosaur are made by a scientific body named the International Commission on Zoological Nomenclature, usually known as ICZN. The 25 members of the ICZN are elected by respected zoologists from countries across the world.

⬆ *The gigantic* Brachiosaurus *was one of the heaviest dinosaurs that ever lived. Several different sorts of this dinosaur have been found by scientists, and there has been much confusion over the names that should be used to describe them.*

Are sauropod remains still being found?

Yes, the sauropods *Jobaria* and *Janenschia* were discovered in Africa during the 1990s. Only parts of the skeletons of these huge dinosaurs were found, so scientists have had to reconstruct these animals by comparing them to other sauropods. *Jobaria* was about 70 ft. long and weighed around 20 tons. *Janenschia* was slightly smaller. What may be another new type of sauropod was found in America in 2004, but it has not yet been properly studied.

What did sauropods eat?

The teeth of sauropods are fairly small and usually blunt, which shows that they must have eaten plants. Sauropods would have needed to eat vast amounts of plant food to gain enough energy for their huge bodies. These dinosaurs became much rarer after about 100 million years ago, so perhaps the plants that they ate began to disappear. Scientists know that flowering plants began to appear at this time, so ferns became rarer than they had been.

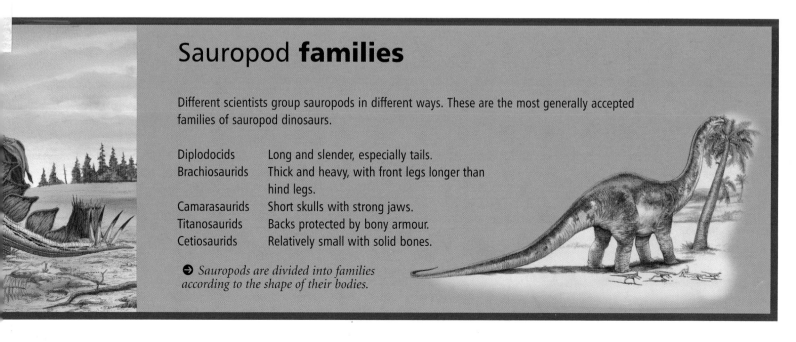

Sauropod **families**

Different scientists group sauropods in different ways. These are the most generally accepted families of sauropod dinosaurs.

Diplodocids	Long and slender, especially tails.
Brachiosaurids	Thick and heavy, with front legs longer than hind legs.
Camarasaurids	Short skulls with strong jaws.
Titanosaurids	Backs protected by bony armour.
Cetiosaurids	Relatively small with solid bones.

➔ *Sauropods are divided into families according to the shape of their bodies.*

Dinosaurs have left behind them large numbers of fossils of their teeth and bones, but very few of the muscles, organs, and other features have been preserved. Scientists have tried to work out what the soft parts of dinosaurs were like by comparing the skeletons with those of animals that are alive today. We now have a fairly complete idea of what the insides of a dinosaur would have looked like.

🔼 *The astonishingly long necks of sauropod dinosaurs evolved to help these creatures find and eat the large quantities of food needed to keep their massive bodies going.*

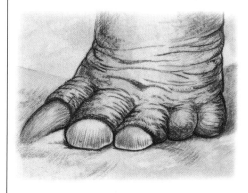

🔼 *Footprints are left behind in mud or sand, but soon disappear. They are fossilized under only the rarest of conditions.*

How did sauropods eat?

Sauropods had to eat vast amounts of plant food, but their teeth were quite small and their jaw muscles were weak. The teeth of *Apatosaurus* were long and narrow—like pencils. Experts think *Apatosaurus* may have used its teeth like rakes, grabbing a mouthful of leaves, then pulling its head backwards to remove the leaves from the tree or bush.

Why did sauropods have such long necks?

The long neck allowed sauropods to reach the plant food that they ate. The neck of *Mamenchisaurus* was the longest of any dinosaur. It was about 36 ft. long and made up of just 19 bones. Scientists think that sauropods may have stood still and used their necks to enable them to gather food from a large area before moving forwards to the center of a new grazing patch. This would have meant the animal did not need to walk around much and so would have saved energy.

How are footprints fossilized?

Footprints are fossilized only if they are buried in sediment almost as soon as they are made. If a dinosaur made footprints in wet sand on a beach, they might be buried beneath fresh sediments by the incoming tide. Or a flood might lay mud down on top of footprints made on a river bank. Only if the new sediments were different from those in which the footprints were made would the prints become fossilized. This means that fossilized footprints are extremely rare, and also fragile. If the fossils are not excavated within a few weeks and taken to a museum for storage, they are likely to be broken up by frost or washed away by water. Many fossil footprints are lost before they can be studied.

Inside sauropods

🔽 *The brachiosaurid sauropods were the only dinosaurs that had front legs longer than their hind legs.*

- Sauropods swallowed stones called gastroliths to help digest their food.
- Sauropods could lift only one foot at a time when walking as they needed three feet on the ground to support their weight.
- Some sauropods had armor plate made of bone across their backs to protect them from attack.
- Some sauropods had their nostrils on top of their heads, between the eyes.
- *Brachiosaurus* is one of the few dinosaurs to have longer front legs than hind legs.
- Scientists used to think that sauropods lived in swamps and lakes, but now agree that they walked on dry land.
- Sauropods may have used the claws on their front feet to fight off attacks.
- Sauropods did not lay their eggs in nests but in straight lines.

How did sauropods digest their food?

The teeth and jaws of sauropods were too weak to chew up the vast amounts of food the animals ate. Instead, the food was swallowed whole. In the stomach the plants were mashed to a paste by stones, called gastroliths, swallowed by the dinosaur. The bacteria in the stomach broke down the nutrients in the plants so that the dinosaur could digest them. This method of digesting food is used by several modern animals. Some birds keep gravel in their digestive systems to grind up seeds or tough plants, while crocodiles swallow stones to help pound bones to pieces.

The skulls of diplodocid sauropods had only a few short teeth at the front of their mouths, so they were unable to chew their food properly.

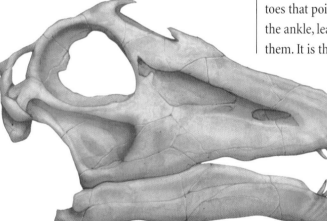

The feet of sauropod dinosaurs were large and wide so that they could carry their heavy weight. Smaller dinosaurs had narrow feet better suited to fast running.

Were sauropod feet special?

Sauropods were enormously heavy, but had to support their weight on their four feet. Each foot was made up of toes that pointed down and outwards from the ankle, leaving an empty space between them. It is thought that this space was filled by strong, soft tissue similar to tendons. This would have cushioned the foot when it was put down, and helped support the great weight of the animal.

The neck bones of sauropod dinosaurs were hollowed out to make them as light as possible so that the animal did not need to use up huge amounts of energy just lifting its head.

Have any complete skeletons been found?

It is very rare that a complete dinosaur skeleton is found. For bones to be fossilized they need to be buried in mud or sand quickly, which doesn't often happen. It is extremely rare to find an entire sauropod skeleton. Most dinosaur fossils consist of just a few bones, though the whole skeletons of some smaller types have been found. This means that many types of dinosaur are known from only part of the skeleton. Scientists have to reconstruct the whole animal when they have direct evidence for only part of it. They do this by looking for a similar dinosaur for which the missing parts have been found. They then adapt the known features to match the missing parts and produce a composite reconstruction.

Dinosaur **fur**

Because dinosaurs were reptiles, scientists thought they had scaly skin like modern reptiles. However, through studying tiny details in newly discovered fossils, scientists have now discovered that some smaller dinosaurs had a fur-like covering that may be related to feathers.

Several smaller dinosaurs such as Sinosauropteryx, *were covered with soft, downy, hair-like structures that may have helped to keep them warm in cold weather. It is thought that these structures were more like short feathers than hair. Only a few fossils with this down have been discovered so scientists are not completely certain what it looked like.*

The Jurassic Period lasted from about 200 to 145 million years ago. During the Jurassic Period the world's climate was much warmer and wetter than at other times. There were no flowering plants at this time, but the land was covered by lush growth of ferns and other plants. The largest animals were the sauropod dinosaurs, but there were many different types of dinosaurs and other animals as well.

⬆ *Ichthyosaurs were reptiles that were adapted to life in the sea.*

Which were the first large ornithischian dinosaurs?

For millions of years the ornithischian dinosaurs remained small and fairly rare. Then, about 160 million years ago, a new family of ornithischians appeared. These were the stegosaurids and they spread across the world in large numbers. After around 50 million years of success, the stegosaurids died out and were replaced by other types of dinosaur. The largest was *Stegosaurus*, which grew to be about 23 ft. long and lived in North America.

⬇ *Stegosaurus was a massive creature armed with sharp spikes on its tail. It was a plant-eater that used its weapons for defense.*

What animals lived in Jurassic seas?

During the Jurassic Period there were many different sorts of fish, but the largest animals were reptiles. Large areas of what is now land were flooded in Jurassic times by warm, shallow seas. Among the reptiles that lived here were turtles up to 13 ft. long. Plesiosaurs had long necks so they could snap up fish in their jaws. Ichthyosaurs were reptiles that swam like fish.

Small **dinosaurs**

⬇ *There were several families of very small dinosaurs. The Compsognathids were the size of a modern chicken.*

- *Heterodontosaurus* was named for the three different types of teeth in its mouth. It ate plants in Africa about 180 million years ago.
- *Lesothosaurus* was 3 ft. long and ate plants. It lived in southern Africa 190 million years ago.
- The plant-eater *Othnielia* from North America lived 140 million years ago was just 4.5 ft. long.
- *Compsognathus* was a tiny hunter from Europe 140 million years ago. It was just 35 in. long.
- *Ornitholestes* was 6.5 ft. long. It was a hunter that lived in North America 145 million years ago.

⬆ *The crests of* Dilophosaurus *are a mystery.*

Why did hunting dinosaurs have crests?

Scientists are not certain why several of the large, meat-eating dinosaurs had crests or horns of bone growing from their skulls. The most likely explanation is that the crests were used to signal to other dinosaurs of the same type, but they may have helped the dinosaur sight on prey or have contained special glands of some kind.

Which animals lived in the early Jurassic Period?

The early part of the Jurassic Period saw a group of dinosaurs called prosauropods roam the Earth. Prosauropods all died out about 160 million years ago, though one group then evolved into sauropod dinosaurs. The largest prosauropods were about 26 ft. long. They ate plants and most could run on their hind legs for short bursts.

Why did *Stegosaurus* have back plates?

The large plates of bone that grew from the back of *Stegosaurus* and other stegosaurid dinosaurs may have had more than one purpose. The skin covering the plates was filled with large blood vessels. If *Stegosaurus* was too hot, it could fill these with blood to cool down. Or it could stand in the sun and soak up warmth if it was too cold. The skin may also have been able to change color, like that of some modern reptiles, allowing *Stegosaurus* to signal to others of its kind.

Was *Stegosaurus* stupid?

The brain of *Stegosaurus* was tiny – it had the smallest brain for its size of any dinosaur. The brain was only about 2 in. long while the complete animal was over 23 ft. This may indicate that *Stegosaurus* was not very smart, but it was obviously smart enough as it managed to survive for several million years. There was a large mass of nerves located in the hips, which some scientists believe may have controlled the movements of the legs and tail, so the brain did not have to do this job.

⬇ Riojasaurus *was a prosauropod that lived in South America right at the start of the Jurassic Period.*

Ages of the Jurassic **Period**

All dates are approximate
Millions of years ago

Millions of years ago	Age
201.9	Hettangian
195.3	Sinemurian
189.6	Pliensbachian
180.1	Toarcian
176.5	Aalenian
169.2	Bajocian
164.4	Bathonian
159.4	Callovian
154.1	Oxfordian
150.7	Kimmeridgian
144.2	Tithonian

⬇ Heterodontosaurus *lived only during the Hettangian, so if scientists find these bones they know exactly how old the rocks are.*

The skies above the dinosaurs were filled with flying animals, but they were very different from modern birds. First to take to the air were the pterosaurs, or winged reptiles. These creatures were archosaurs, and therefore related to the dinosaurs, evolving into hundreds of different types. Later, the birds appeared, probably having evolved from a small type of dinosaur about 170 million years ago.

⊙ *The flying reptiles, or pterosaurs, dominated the skies for tens of millions of years. They evolved into a wide variety of forms in all shapes and sizes.*

Which animal was the first to fly?

Several different sorts of reptiles were able to glide from tree to tree, but the first vertebrate able to fly properly was a pterosaur. One of the earliest pterosaurs was *Rhamphorhynchus*, which had a wingspan of about 5 ft. and lived 180 million years ago in Europe. Like all early pterosaurs it had a long tail with a small flap of skin at the end. This may have acted like the rudder on an aircraft, enabling the animal to change direction in flight.

Which was the largest pterosaur?

***Quetzalcoatlus* of North America was the largest pterosaur and also the largest flying animal ever known.** *Quetzalcoatlus* had a wingspan of about 40 ft. and weighed an amazing 220 pounds. As far as is known, it probably flew slowly, soaring on air currents while looking for food. The animal is named after Quetzalcoatl, a god of the Aztec people of Mexico. The god was said to have had the appearance of a snake and was covered in feathers.

Were all pterosaurs alike?

No, because over the millions of years that pterosaurs existed they gradually changed and evolved dramatically. The earliest pterosaurs lived about 230 million years ago. They were small, agile flyers with long bony tails. The latest pterosaurs lived 65 million years ago and were huge, soaring creatures. However, the wings of all the pterosaurs were composed of leathery flaps of skin supported by fourth fingers, which had evolved to be extremely long.

Which was the first bird?

***Archaeopteryx* was the earliest known bird—its name meant "ancient wing."** It lived in Europe about 150 million years ago, and had feathers that were laid out exactly as in modern birds. *Archaeopteryx* was probably able to fly short distances. It was about 18 in. long and may have hunted insects and small creatures in a forested area. Because it lacked strong muscles attached to its wings, it was probably not a very good flyer.

⊙ *Archaeopteryx swoops down from a branch to catch an insect. With feathered wings, this creature was better suited than a pterosaur to flying among trees in a forest, with its easily damaged wings of skin.*

Taking to the **skies**

Key **dates**

Millions of years ago

230	Probable date of first pterosaur.
220	Oldest known pterosaur: *Eudimorphodon,* which lived in Europe.
200	Oldest known American pterosaur: *Dimorphodon.*
190	Oldest known Asian pterosaur: *Campylognathoides.*
155	Oldest known pterosaur without a tail: *Pterodactylus.*
145	Last known pterosaur with a tail: *Sordes.*
70	Largest known pterosaur: *Quetzalcoatlus.*
65	Last known pterosaur: *Nyctosaurus.*

⊙ *A pair of pterosaurs soar across the sky during the age of the dinosaurs.*

What did the ancestor of birds look like?

Most scientists think that birds are descended from a small hunting dinosaur of some kind. This little creature probably looked like the *Protoarchaeopteryx*, which was about the size of a modern turkey and was covered in feathers. The front legs of *Protoarchaeopteryx* were not strong enough to be used as wings, but were longer than those of most small hunting dinosaurs.

➲ *Sinosauropteryx was a hunting dinosaur that was covered in feathers. The name means "Chinese lizard wing."*

Did only birds have feathers?

No, several different types of small dinosaur were also covered in feathers. The first dinosaur to be found which had fossilized feathers was *Sinosauropteryx*, which lived about 125 million years ago in China. This small hunter was 4 ft. long and was covered in small feathers. It probably used the feathers to help it keep warm.

How did the birds evolve?

After the time of *Archaeopteryx*, birds evolved slowly, but by about 80 million years ago birds were the most numerous flying vertebrates. The pterosaurs were becoming much rarer than they had been. *Ichthyornis* was a small seabird that was a good flier and probably hunted fish in the open ocean.

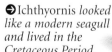

➲ *Ichthyornis looked like a modern seagull and lived in the Cretaceous Period.*

Five largest flying animals **ever**

Name	Place	Time	Wingspan
Quetzalcoatlus	North America	late Cretaceous	40 ft.
Pteranodon	North America	mid-Cretaceous	30 ft.
Tropeognathus	South America	mid-Cretaceous	21 ft.
Cearadactylus	South America	mid-Cretaceous	18 ft.
Ornithodesmus	Europe	early Cretaceous	16 ft.

About 85 million years ago a new type of dinosaur evolved—the ceratopsids, or horned dinosaurs. At first these animals were quite small, around 6 ft. long, but they rapidly evolved to become larger. The largest ceratopsid was *Triceratops*, which grew to over 30 ft. in length. By 65 million years ago these were among the most numerous of all dinosaurs.

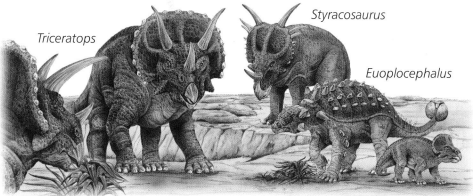

Triceratops

Styracosaurus

Euoplocephalus

Protoceratops

↑ *Armored and horned dinosaurs became more common in the Cretaceous Period.*

How many types of horned dinosaur were there?

Scientists have identified about 30 types of horned dinosaur, but there were probably many others that have not been found yet. The earliest were quite small and had no horns, such as *Protoceratops*, which lived in Asia about 85 million years ago. Later ones were larger and had several horns, such as *Styracosaurus* from North America 80 million years ago. Dinosaurs that had armor, such as *Euoplocephalus,* lived at the same time.

Why were the horned dinosaurs so successful?

The horned dinosaurs became numerous and widespread because of their teeth and jaws. The large frills at the back of the skull allowed for powerful muscles to work the jaws, which were filled with dozens of sharp slicing teeth. Ceratopsids were able to slice up and swallow large quantities of tough plant food that other dinosaurs could not eat.

How large were the eggs?

The eggs of *Protoceratops* were nearly 8 in. long and were oval in shape. Most of the eggs were laid in nests that had been scooped out of the ground. The eggs were laid in circles lining the nest and were sometimes piled up on top of each other. Each nest contained between 12 and 18 eggs.

↓ *Protoceratops eggs were shaped like long ovals. This may have stopped them rolling off the edges of the nest.*

↓ *Like other horned dinosaurs,* Protoceratops *had a beak at the front of its jaws to nip leaves from plants and teeth at the rear to chew food.*

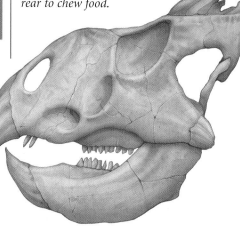

Horned **history**

Key **dates**

Millions of years ago

95	Possible ancestor of later horned dinosaurs lived in eastern Asia: *Psittacosaurus*.
85	Oldest known horned dinosaur with neck frill lived in Asia: *Protoceratops*.
80	Oldest known horned dinosaur with horns lived in western North America: *Brachyceratops*.
78	Oldest known long-frilled horned dinosaur lived in western North America: *Chasmosaurus*.
65	Last horned dinosaur: *Triceratops*.

↑ *Psittacosaurus was an early horned dinosaur that had not yet evolved horns.*

Which was one of the most famous fossil discoveries?

In 1922 an American expedition travelled to the Gobi Desert in central Asia (Mongolia) to search for fossils of ancient humans. Instead they found hundreds of dinosaur fossils. One of these was a complete nest, together with eggs and mother. The dinosaur was *Protoceratops,* and this proved for the first time that dinosaurs laid eggs and that the mother looked after the nest. It took the expedition months to excavate the find and carry news to the outside world. When the fossils reached America, they caused a sensation. Soon, other expeditions were sent to the Gobi Desert to look for more nests, but only a few were found.

⊙ *Protoceratops guards its nest of eggs. The eggs would probably have been buried under piles of leaves. As the leaves rotted they gave off heat that kept the eggs warm.*

Did dinosaurs migrate?

It is likely that at least some dinosaurs moved from one area to another as the seasons changed, just as modern birds and mammals do. If plants grew well in one place during the summer, but in another during the winter, the horned dinosaurs that fed on them would have moved to feed. Horned dinosaurs such as *Centrosaurus* lived in herds and would have migrated in search of food. So far there is little direct evidence that dinosaurs behaved in this way, though fossils of the forest dinosaur *Plateosaurus* have been found in what was then a desert. It may very well have been migrating between forests when it died.

⊙ *Triceratops uses its horns to fight off an attack by* Tyrannosaurus. *The long, sharp horns would have been able to inflict a serious injury on the hunter, but the flanks and tail of* Triceratops *were vulnerable to attack and would have been easy targets.*

Were the horns good weapons?

Horned dinosaurs had long, sharp horns that grew from their skulls and were used as powerful weapons. *Triceratops* had three extremely sharp horns, which may have been used to fight off attacks from hunting dinosaurs, such as *Tyrannosaurus*. They may also have been used to settle disputes between rival horned dinosaurs fighting over feeding grounds or to see who would lead the herd.

Amazing **facts**

- *Torosaurus* had one the largest skulls of any land animal—it was over 8 ft. long.
- Some horned dinosaurs did not have horns, such as the early *Psittacosaurus* that lived in Asia about 95 million years ago.
- Horned dinosaurs became more numerous as flowering plants spread, so some scientists think they were good at eating these new plants.
- The different types of horned dinosaur are distinguished by their horn shapes.
- The large neck frills may have been brightly colored and used to threaten other dinosaurs.
- The horned dinosaur *Monoclonius* is known only from very few fossils.
- *Styracosaurus* had horns pointing backward from the head instead of forward.

➲ *It is thought that the success of the horned dinosaurs was due to the plants they ate.*

Around 100 million years ago a new group of dinosaurs evolved in Asia. Hadrosaurs were all large, plant-eating dinosaurs, which could walk on all four legs or on just two. Hadrosaurs were closely related to *Iguanodon*, but had webbed feet and slightly different sorts of teeth. Scientists have so far found over 40 types of hadrosaur, all of which lived between 100 and 65 million years ago in Asia, North America, and South America.

⬆ *Faint marks on the jaws of hadrosaurs show that these animal had cheek muscles.*

Why were hadrosaurs special?

The jaws of hadrosaurs contained hundreds of teeth, which were packed very tightly together. When a hadrosaur closed its mouth, the upper jaws slid outwards over the lower jaws. As the teeth ground past each other they would have reduced any plant food to a mushy pulp. This made the food easy to digest and allowed hadrosaurs to feed on plants that other dinosaurs could not eat.

Did all hadrosaurs have crests?

Many species of hadrosaur did not have crests of any sort on top of their heads. *Anatosaurus* was over 33 ft. long and weighed over 3 tons. Like other hadrosaurs it had strong muscles attached to its tail, which it may have used for swimming.

Which was the oddest hadrosaur?

The hadrosaur dinosaurs are famous for having strange bony crests, but the largest crest by far was that on *Parasaurolophus*, which was over 3 ft. long. Scientists believe the crests were covered with colorful skin and were used as a way of signalling to other dinosaurs of the same species. They may have been used to frighten off rivals or to attract mates.

⬇ *Hadrosaurs were probably able to swim well, and it is thought that they may have plunged into deep water to escape from packs of hunting dinosaurs.*

Anatosaurus

Velociraptors

Hadrosaur **facts**

Key **dates**

Millions of years ago

110	Probable date of the first hadrosaur to evolve from an iguanodontid.
100	Oldest known hadrosaur: *Bactrosaurus* in eastern Asia.
90	Oldest known hadrosaur in North America: *Corythosaurus*.
65	Last known hadrosaur: *Parasaurolophus* in North America.

➔ *The large, angular headcrest shows this is a male* Corythosaurus.

How did hadrosaurs care for their young?

Adult hadrosaurs brought food to the nests for their young. The fossils show that young hadrosaurs stayed in the nest for several months after hatching. This allowed the adults to feed them and also to protect them from danger.

How did hadrosaurs build their nests?

Hadrosaurs built nests by digging earth into a round mound. In 1978, a colony of fossilized hadrosaur nests, belonging to the dinosaur *Maiasaura*, was found in Montana. This showed that hadrosaurs built their nests close together.

⊙ Many scientists think that hadrosaurs such as Parasaurolophus *lived close to water for most of their lives. They probably ate both water plants and plants that grew on land.*

⊙ Fossils of the hadrosaur dinosaur Maiasaura *included nests, eggs, babies after hatching, and broken eggshells.*

❸ This Maiasaura *egg is pointed, so that it fitted closely with other eggs in the nest.*

Why are hadrosaurs called "duck-bills"?

The front of the mouth of hadrosaur dinosaurs was wide and flat, like that of a modern duck, so some people call these the "duck-billed dinosaurs." However, the beaks of the hadrosaurs were strong, sharp, and worked by powerful muscles, unlike the soft, weak bills on ducks.

Strange crests

Scientists have come up with several ideas to explain the strange crests on hadrosaurs. Here are five ideas that nobody believes any longer!

- Hadrosaurs stored air in the crests when diving underwater.
- Hadrosaurs had special glands in the crest for getting rid of salt.
- The crests contained huge amounts of scent pores to give the hadrosaurs a very good sense of smell.
- The crests helped push branches out the way when the hadrosaur walked through a forest.
- The crests were used like snorkels, so the hadrosaur could breathe underwater.

⊙ *The dramatic crests of* Parasaurolophus *may have served more than one function.*

Among the rarest dinosaur fossils are those of the armored dinosaurs. Very few of these fossils have been found, and usually only part of the dinosaur is preserved as a fossil. The armored dinosaurs existed from 180 million years ago until 65 million years ago and are found on most continents, so they were a successful group. Perhaps they lived in areas where fossils did not form very easily, such as in mountainous regions.

Which dinosaur had the most armor?

The most heavily armored dinosaur was *Ankylosaurus,* which lived in North America about 70 million years ago. The entire back of the body was covered by plates of solid bone, while spikes and knobs stuck out at odd angles. The head was covered by thick sheets of bone and even the eyelid had a covering of bone armor.

How did *Ankylosaurus* live?

The armored *Ankylosaurus* was a large plant-eating dinosaur that grew to be over 36 ft. long and stood almost 10 ft. tall. The legs were strong, but solid, so the animal probably walked quite slowly. Its teeth were adapted to eating plants, but the jaw muscles were weak so *Ankylosaurus* must have eaten quite soft plants.

⊙*A* Spinosaurus *attacks an* Ankylosaur. *The armored dinosaur is fighting back with the heavy club on the end of its tail.*

How did *Ankylosaurus* defend itself?

The *Ankylosaurus*'s main defense against attack was the armor that covered its body, but it had a more impressive weapon it could use. At the end of its tail was a huge mass of solid bone. *Ankylosaurus* may have used its powerful tail muscles to swing this heavy weight at an attacker. The tail club used like this could have seriously injured even the largest hunting dinosaur.

Awesome **armor**

Key **dates**

Millions of years ago

180	Possible ancestor of armored dinosaurs: *Sarcolestes* in Great Britain.
125	Oldest known armored dinosaur: *Hylaeosaurus* in Great Britain.
110	Probable ancestor of bone-head dinosaurs: *Yaverlandia* in Europe.
107	Oldest known ankylosaur: *Sauroplites* in Asia.
85	Oldest known bone-head dinosaur: *Stegoceras* in North America.
65	Last known ankylosaur: *Ankylosaurus* in North America.
65	Last known bone-head dinosaur: *Pachycephalosaurus* in North America.

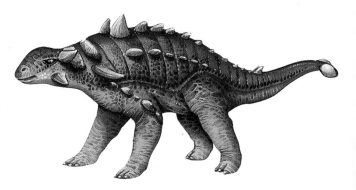

⊙*Armored dinosaurs often had knobs or spikes of bone growing from their armor as an added defense.*

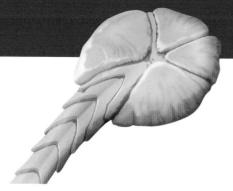

⬆ *The club on the end of Ankylosaurus's tail contained several large bones fused together.*

What were the bone-head dinosaurs?

Bone-head dinosaurs are properly called pachycephalosaurs, and were dinosaurs with skulls that were topped by massively thick layers of solid bone. *Stegoceras* lived in North America about 70 million years ago and was 6.5 ft. long. Like other pachycephalosaurs, it ate plants and walked on its two hind legs.

Which was the smallest bone-head dinosaur?

The smallest of the pachycephalosaurs so far known to scientists was *Wannanosaurus*, which lived in China about 70 million years ago. *Wannanosaurus* was only 2 ft. long. The largest of the pachycephalosaurs was *Pachycephalosaurus* which grew to be over 26 ft. long. The size of most other forms of bone-head is unclear as the bodies are rarely fossilized intact. Only the thick bone of the skull is usually found.

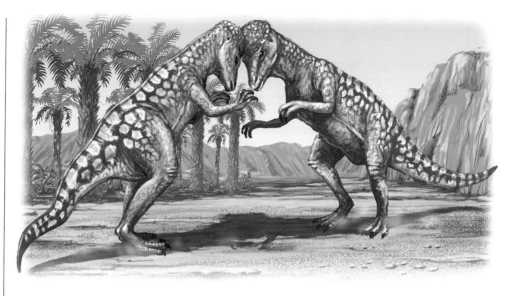

⬆ *A pair of large* Pachycephalosaurus *strike each other during a conflict. These were the largest of the bone-head dinosaurs measuring 26 ft. in length.*

Why did bone-heads have such thick skulls?

The pachycephalosaurs used their heads to fight with. When two *Stegoceras* fought, they would lower their heads and charge straight at each other. When the two animals collided, their heads would crash into each other with great force, but the thick bones stopped them from being seriously injured. Eventually, the weaker animal would give up and lose the fight.

⬇ *The butting could be very fierce, but after several clashes the weaker bone-head dinosaur would give up the fight and retreat.*

Amazing **facts**

- *Pachycephalosaurus* had the thickest skull bone of any creature—over 10 in.
- The fossils of most bone-head dinosaurs consist only of skulls, no other part of the body being found.
- The longest dinosaur name belongs to the bone-head *Micropachycephalosaurus*— 23 letters and 9 syllables.
- The fossils of *Hylaeosaurus* were found in 1833, but have not yet been studied.
- The smallest armored dinosaur was *Struthiosaurus*, which was just 6.5 ft. long.
- When scientists first found the fossils of the armored dinosaur *Sarcolestes*, they thought it was a meat-eater.
- The armored dinosaur *Cryptodraco* was named from a single bone that was found in England.

⬇ Pachycephalosaurus *means "thick-headed reptile," due to the domed and hugely thickened bone that characterizes this kind of dinosaur.*

The Cretaceous Period saw more different types of dinosaur than any other time in history. Among the most impressive were the hunting dinosaurs, which preyed on the plant-eaters of the time. All these hunters were saurischian dinosaurs that had replaced earlier *Coelophysis*, *Dilophosaurus* and similar creatures. They varied greatly in size from barely 6 ft. long to giants that were the largest carnivores ever to walk the Earth.

⬆ Troodon *was a fast, agile hunter that used its superior brain power to track down or ambush prey.*

Which was the brainiest dinosaur?

The dinosaur that had the largest brain in relation to its body size was ***Troodon.*** This small, agile hunter lived in North America about 75 million years ago and may have been about as intelligent as a modern parrot. The parts of the brain related to sight were particularly large, so it probably had very good eyesight.

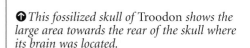

⬆ *This fossilized skull of* Troodon *shows the large area towards the rear of the skull where its brain was located.*

⬆ *A pack of* Deinonychus *attacks a plant-eating* Tenontosaurus. *Only by acting together could hunters bring down prey larger than themselves.*

Did dinosaurs hunt in packs?

Some of the smaller hunters, such as *Deinonychus*, probably worked together to kill larger plant-eaters that a single hunter could not tackle alone. *Tenontosaurus* was a plant-eater that grew to about 20 ft. long. A single *Deinonychus* could not bring it down, but several hunters attacking at the same time could overwhelm an animal of this size. Such cooperation required larger brains so that they could understand what the others were doing.

On the **hunt**

Amazing **facts**

- *Baryonyx* had its nostrils set back from its snout, possibly so it could dip its jaws into water to catch fish.
- Most of the smaller hunters were covered with feathers to help them keep warm.
- The name *Troodon* means "wounding tooth."
- Scientists cannot agree about how to group the hunters of the Cretaceous Period—some put dinosaurs in one group, others in a different group.
- All Cretaceous Period hunters have three claws on their hind feet facing forwards and one smaller claw pointing backwards.

⬇ *Ostrich dinosaurs such as* Dromiceiomimus *lived towards the end of the Cretaceous Period in North America and Asia.*

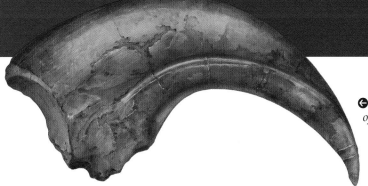

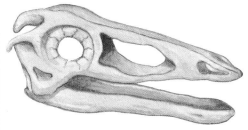

The fiercely curved claw of Deinonychus *measured 5 in. long, but would have been even longer with its horny covering.*

This skull of Ornithomimus *shows that it had no teeth in its jaws.*

Which dinosaur ate fish?

The dinosaur *Baryonyx* probably ate fish, not other dinosaurs. The mouth of *Baryonyx* was filled with a large number of small, sharp teeth. These were ideal for gripping slippery objects, such as fish. The front legs of the dinosaur were equipped with curved claws to hook fish from the water. The shoulders of this dinosaur were unusually powerful, so it could use its very large thumb claw to capture large creatures. *Baryonyx* lived in Great Britain about 120 million years ago and grew to be 36 ft. long.

Which dinosaur is called the "Mystery Killer"?

In 1970 scientists from Poland found two mysterious fossilized dinosaur arms in the Gobi Desert, which they called *Deinocheirus* meaning "Terrible Hand." The arms were over 6 ft. long and carried razor-sharp claws about 11 in. long. Nobody knows what the rest of the dinosaur looked like as only the arms have been found—so it is a mystery killer.

What was the "Terrible Claw"?

The name of the dinosaur *Deinonychus* means "Terrible Claw." It got its name from the ferocious hooked claw on its hind legs. Located on the second toe, the claw could be flicked back and forwards very quickly. These claws were vicious weapons of attack and could cause terrible injuries.

A pair of racing Ornithomimus. *Scientists are unsure of the lifestyle of this dinosaur.*

Which hunters had no teeth?

The ornithomimids—a group of hunting dinosaurs. *Ornithomimus* was about 11 ft. long, but weighed only 330 pounds. It was very light for its size, with long legs that made it a fast runner. This dinosaur may have eaten insects, eggs, or other food that did not require teeth for feeding.

Key dates

The Cretaceous Period is divided into a number of ages as follows:

All dates are approximate
Millions of years ago

137	Berriasian	93.5	Cenomanian
132	Valanginian	89.9	Turonian
127.0	Hauterivian	85.8	Coniacian
121.0	Barremian	83.5	Santonian
112.2	Aptian	71	Campanian
98.9	Albian	65	Maastrichtian

Some Cretaceous hunters had strong claws on their hind feet and are grouped as a single family.

One of the most famous dinosaurs is *Tyrannosaurus rex*, a huge meat-eating creature from the very end of the Cretaceous Period about 65 million years ago. Some scientists think that *Tyrannosaurus* was powerful enough to hunt and kill the largest plant-eating dinosaurs of the time. Other scientists think that it was too slow to catch prey and that it fed on dinosaurs that had died a natural death instead.

What did *Tyrannosaurus rex* look like?

Tyrannosaurus rex walked on its hind legs only, with its powerful tail balancing the weight of its body and head. It was a muscular animal that had a large mouth filled with long, sharp teeth and a jaw so wide it made a formidable predator.

⬇Tyrannosaurus *had large, pointed teeth that were very strong.*

⬆*Fossilized footprints can show scientists how fast the dinosaur was moving.*

How fast could *Tyrannosaurus rex* move?

Scientists think that *Tyrannosaurus* was a fairly active dinosaur. It had stout, muscular legs that could not move quickly, but they were long enough to cover quite a distance with each step. It may have been able to reach 20 mi./hr., but only for short bursts of time. More usually it would have walked at about 3 mi./hr.

What dinosaurs did *Tyrannosaurus rex* eat?

At the time that *Tyrannosaurus* lived in North America, there were large numbers of plant-eating dinosaurs called hadrosaurs, on which *Tyrannosaurus* probably preyed. *Tyrannosaurus* may also have fed on horned dinosaurs, which also existed at this time, though their horns may have made them more difficult to kill. It would certainly have fed on large plant-eaters so it got enough to eat at each meal.

➡*A* Tyrannosaurus *towers over a young* Parasaurolophus. *Many scientists think the hunter ambushed its prey rather than chasing it for long distances.*

Tyrannosaurus **relatives**

⬆*The Asian* Tarbosaurus *was almost identical to* Tyrannosaurus.

Tarbosaurus	Lived in central Asia about 70 million years ago. Grew to reach 40 ft. in length and weighed 5 tons.
Daspletosaurus	Lived in North America about 75 million years ago. Grew to about 30 ft. in length and weighed 3 tons.
Shanshanosaurus	Lived in China about 70 million years ago. Grew to 10 ft. in length.
Aublysodon	Lived in North America about 70 million years ago. Grew over 16 ft. in length and weighed 220 lbs.
Gorgosaurus	Lived in North America about 74 million years ago. Grew to about 30 ft. in length and weighed 3 tons.
Albertosaurus	Lived in North America about 73 million years ago. Grew to over 26 ft. in length and weighed about 2 tons.

Why were its arms so small?

The arms of *Tyrannosaurus* might have been used to help it stand up.
Tyrannosaurus had tiny arms, just over 3 ft. long compared to its overall length of about 42 ft. It is thought that *Tyrannosaurus* lay on its stomach when resting, because very strong bones have been found along the chest and the stomach that may have helped support it when it was lying down. When standing up it could have braced itself using its small front legs, and heaving itself up using its powerful leg muscles.

⬆ *Tyrannosaurus may have lived in forests and hunted in packs.*

Why was its skull so strong?

The skull of *Tyrannosaurus* may have been so strong because of the hunting technique it used. *Tyrannosaurus* had a skull that was reinforced by strong pieces of bone at the main pressure points. Some scientists think it may have attacked prey by running at them with its jaws wide open. This would inflict a terrible blow on the victim, but *Tyrannosaurus* would have been protected from injury by its strong skull.

Was *Tyrannosaurus rex* the biggest hunter dinosaur?

No, the largest meat-eating dinosaur so far found by scientists was *Giganotosaurus*. This dinosaur was about 50 ft. long and may have weighed up to 9 tons, more than 2 tons heavier than *Tyrannosaurus*. It is thought that *Giganotosaurus* may have hunted the sauropod dinosaurs that survived in South America longer than elsewhere. Only a few fossils of *Giganotosaurus* have been found, so it is not as well-known as *Tyrannosaurus*.

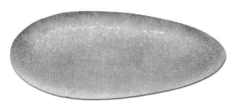

⬆ *The eggs of big meat-eaters like* Tyrannosaurus *were almost 16 in. long and 6 in. wide.*

Key **dates**

1850	Several large fossil teeth are found in Montana.
1856	Some of these teeth are named as *Deinodon*. No other body parts are found.
1869	Different teeth from the same group are named *Aublysodon*.
1902	A fossil skeleton with teeth similar to earlier finds is excavated in Montana.
1905	The new find is described as *Tyrannosaurus rex*. The earlier teeth are recognized as belonging to similar dinosaurs.
1905	The first fossils of *Albertosaurus* are discovered.
1914	*Gorgosaurus* fossils are found for the first time.
1955	Fossils of *Tarbosaurus* are found.
1970	Fossils of *Daspletosaurus* are discovered.
1977	Fossils of *Shanshanosaurus* are found for the first time.

Some time around 65 million years ago the dinosaurs disappeared. Rocks older than this date are filled with the fossils of different types of dinosaurs, but younger rocks contain no dinosaurs. The reason why a group of animals that had dominated the world for over 160 million years should vanish so completely has puzzled scientists ever since the dinosaurs were first discovered. There have been many different theories to explain the event.

➊ *The collision of a gigantic meteorite would have killed all dinosaurs near the impact immediately, but all life on Earth would have been affected within a few weeks.*

➋ *Vast volcanic eruptions are known to have taken place about the time the dinosaurs died out.*

What was the world like just before the extinction?

About 66 million years ago the world was dominated by dinosaurs. In Asia and North America there was a wide variety of armored dinosaurs, horned dinosaurs, hadrosaurs, and hunting dinosaurs. Elsewhere, there were sauropods, stegosaurs, and various meat-eaters. Some of these animals existed in large numbers, and all of them seemed to be thriving. There was no sign that a disaster was about to happen.

Did the dinosaurs die out all at once?

Scientists who study the extinction of the dinosaurs are not certain if the event happened in a single year or over a period of several thousand years. The rocks that contain the fossils cannot be dated accurately enough to give this information. However, we do know that dinosaurs all over the planet died out at the same time. Whatever caused the extinction affected every part of the world.

Could a meteor have killed the dinosaurs?

It is thought that if a large meteorite hit the planet, it would throw up a dense cloud of dust and water that would block sunlight from the Earth's surface for several months. This would cause plants to die off, which in turn would cause the death of most types of animal, which could have included dinosaurs.

Animals becoming extinct

Existing animals by the end of the Cretaceous Period	Surviving animals after the end of the Cretaceous Period
Dinosaurs	Mammals
Plesiosaur sea reptiles	Birds
Ichthyosaur sea reptiles	Freshwater crocodiles
Pterosaur flying reptiles	Tortoises
Lepidosaur reptiles	Lizards
Sea crocodiles	Most forms of shellfish
Ammonite shellfish	Most forms of plankton
Chalky plankton	

➋ *Marine crocodiles are just one of several groups of animals that died out at the same time as the dinosaurs.*

Could mammals have wiped out the dinosaurs?

One theory that nobody takes seriously any longer is that the mammals may have wiped out the dinosaurs. It was said that the small mammals of the late Cretaceous Period were adapted for eating eggs. If they ate enough dinosaur eggs, they would have wiped out the dinosaurs by stopping them producing any young. However, there do not seem to have been enough mammals to have achieved this. In any case, if the egg-eating mammals ate all the dinosaur eggs, then they would have destroyed their own source of food, which means they would have died out themselves.

What happened after the dinosaurs?

After the dinosaurs vanished from the Earth, the world still had many kinds of animals. The creatures that survived included mammals, birds, insects, lizards, and other small creatures. It would be many years before these animals evolved to become larger and more powerful. However, as time passed, the mammals began to inhabit and thrive in the world once governed by the dinosaurs. Today, the world is dominated by mammals in much the same way that it was once dominated by dinosaurs. Nonetheless, there is no modern land animal that is as large as the largest dinosaur would have been.

Did volcanoes have an effect?

About 65 million years ago, volcanic eruptions were taking place that may have caused the death of the dinosaurs. These eruptions were larger than any today, covering thousands of square miles of land with lava. Gas and dust thrown up would have affected the climate, which may have been enough to wipe out the dinosaurs.

⊙ *Within a few million years of the death of the dinosaurs, the world was filled with new types of animals such as crocodiles, snakes, and birds.*

Four major mass **extinctions**

Vendian Extinction — About 560 million years ago around 75 percent of all types of plant and animals on Earth vanished.

Permian Extinction — About 225 million years ago around 70 percent of all species of animal living in the seas suddenly became extinct.

Cretaceous Extinction — About 65 million years ago most of the land animals and several groups of sea animals became extinct. Dinosaurs died out at this time.

Modern Extinction — Over the past 10,000 years many larger land animals such as mammoths, moas, and deer have become extinct as humans hunted them and turned their homes into farmland.

⊙ *The woolly mammoth was numerous 50,000 years ago, but is now extinct. It may have been wiped out by human hunters.*

Why not test your knowledge of dinosaurs! Try answering these questions to find out how much you know about their hunting techniques, biology, diet, habitat, and defenses, as well as fossils, paleontology, and much more. Questions are grouped into the subject areas covered within the pages of this book. See how much you remember, and discover how much more you can learn by looking at other sources to help you answer these questions.

1 Which fish have outlived dinosaurs, hardly developing over millions of years?

Studying the Past

2 What are scientists who study dinosaurs called?
3 Which two parts of a dinosaur are most often found as fossils?
4 What are coprolites?

What were Dinosaurs?

5 What does the word "dinosaur" mean?
6 What are the two groups into which all dinosaurs are classified?
7 Did dinosaurs lay eggs?

Before the Dinosaurs

8 Did the first fish have skeletons made of bone or cartilage?
9 Where does the Coelacanth fish live today?
10 To which modern animals is the extinct ammonite related?

The First Dinosaurs

11 When did the first dinosaurs live?
12 Where did the first dinosaurs live?
13 Do dinosaurs usually have longer hind legs or fore legs?

The Land of Giants

14 How long was *Seismosaurus*?
15 Where were the fossils of the dinosaur *Jobaria* found?
16 What did the sauropods eat?

Inside a Dinosaur

17 What is a gastrolith?
18 Which dinosaur had the longest neck?
19 Did sauropods live only in swamps?

Life in the Jurassic

20 Which reptiles looked like fish and lived in the sea?
21 Where did *Stegosaurus* have a large mass of nerves?
22 How large was *Lesothosaurus*?

Into the Air

23 Did *Rhamphorhynchus* have a long tail?
24 Which was the earliest known bird?
25 How large was the wingspan of *Pteranodon*?

The Horned Dinosaurs

26 Where were the fossilized nests of Protoceratops discovered?
27 Which dinosaur had the largest skull?
28 Did *Psittacosaurus* have horns?

29 In which period did armored and horned dinosaurs become more common?

Hadrosaurs

30 When did hadrosaurs first appear on Earth?

31 How long was the crest of *Parasaurolophus*?

32 Did hadrosaurs store air in their crests when diving underwater?

Bony Dinosaurs

33 Where did *Ankylosaurus* live?

34 What did the bone-head dinosaurs eat?

35 Which dinosaur was named from a single bone?

Cretaceous Hunters

37 How long was *Tenontosaurus*?

38 Where did *Baryonyx* live?

39 Which is the only part of the dinosaur *Deinocheirus* to have been found?

Tyrannosaurus rex

40 Did *Tyrannosaurus* eat hadrosaurs?

41 How long were *Tyrannosaurus* arms?

42 Which relative of *Tyrannosaurus* grew to reach 40 ft. in length and weighed 5 tons?

The End of the Dinosaurs

43 When did the dinosaurs die out?

44 Which was the last period in the Age of the Dinosaurs?

45 Where did massive volcanic eruptions take place about 65 million years ago?

36 What does *Pachycephalosaurus* mean?

Answers

1 Sharks	15 Africa	28 No	42 *Tarbosaurus*
2 Paleontologists	16 Plants	29 Cretaceous Period	43 About 65 million
3 Bones and teeth	17 A stone swallowed by an	30 About 100 million years ago	years ago
4 Fossilized dung	animal to help it digest food	31 About 3 ft.	44 Cretaceous
5 Terrible Lizard	18 *Mamenchisaurus*	32 No	45 India
6 Saurischian and Ornithischian	19 No	33 North America	
7 Yes	20 Ichthyosaurs	34 Plants	
8 Cartilage	21 In its hips	35 *Cryptodraco*	
9 In the Indian Ocean	22 About 3 ft. long	36 Thick-headed reptile	
10 Squid and octopus	23 Yes	37 About 20 ft.	
11 About 230 million years ago	24 *Archaeopteryx*	38 Great Britain	
12 South America	25 About 30 ft.	39 Its arms	
13 Hind legs	26 Mongolia	40 Yes	
14 About 150 ft.	27 *Torosaurus*	41 About 3 ft.	

Page numbers in **bold** refer to main subjects, page numbers in *italics* refer to illustrations.

All artworks are from Miles Kelly artwork bank

All photographs from:
Castrol, CMCD, Corbis, Corel, digitalSTOCK, digitalvision, Flat Earth, Hemera,
ILN, John Foxx, PhotoAlto, PhotoDisc, PhotoEssentials, PhotoPro, Stockbyte